Modern Classics

An Inspector Calls

Louise Machin
Roger Machin

Folens Publishers

Acknowledgements

Editor: Hayley Willer
Illustrations: Lee Sullivan
Cover design: Ed Gallagher
Layout artist: Louise Pellowe
Cover image: Canal + Image UK Ltd.

First published 1999 by Folens Limited, Dunstable and Dublin.
Folens Limited, Albert House, Apex Business Centre, Boscombe Road, Dunstable, LU5 4RL, United Kingdom.

ISBN 1 86202 643–2

Printed in Singapore by Craft Print.

Contents

Teachers' notes

Background

Predictions (Page 6)
This sheet should be used before students have read the play. It asks them to think and talk about the possible outcomes the play may have, based on the information provided about events, characters and themes.

Guess who? (Page 7)
This exercise should be used in conjunction with **'Predictions'** and is a further introduction to the characters, their language and their personalities.

Moral dilemmas (Page 8)
This activity sheet should be completed before students have read the play. It asks them to imagine themselves confronting the situations faced by the characters in *An Inspector Calls* and to consider what they would do in the same situations.

Reading a play (Page 9)
This sheet is to be started when students have read the opening few pages of the play. The idea is for them to be able to consider the unique aspects of drama that make it different from other art forms, particularly prose.

The Inspector's notebook 1, The Inspector's notebook 2 (Pages 10–11)
These sheets provide a framework for students to write summaries of the main events of the play and the roles played by each of the characters. It would be quite possible for students to use these frameworks to fill in information as they read through *An Inspector Calls* and become more familiar with it.

A golden age (Page 12)
This is an exercise that requires some basic research on the years between 1901 and 1914. It is important for providing a historical context to *An Inspector Calls*. It concludes with a comparison between the lives of Eva Smith and Sheila Birling.

The future (Page 13)
Dramatic irony is introduced in a simplified form in this activity. An extension exercise based on Arthur Birling's speech is also given.

Who says? (Page 14)
Students are asked to identify characters through their speech. They should be aware of the fact that often the way somebody says something is as revealing as what they actually say.

Crossword (Page 15)
The crossword can be used as light revision of the main themes and events of the play.

Pre-twentieth century: 'Everyman' (Pages 16–17)
These sheets address the requirement of some exam boards and the interests of good curriculum policy – of wider, pre-twentieth-century reading. The fifteenth-century language of *Everyman* may present problems to some students and it is important that teachers spend time ensuring everyone understands the relatively straightforward concepts it expresses. The parallels between *Everyman* and *An Inspector Calls* are striking, and it is well worth the effort needed.

What happens?

Key episodes: Act 1, Key episodes: Act 2, Key episodes: Act 3 (Pages 18–20)
These sheets ask students to view the main episodes of the play retrospectively and to come to some conclusions about them. They provide a visual and analytical summary of the main events of the play that can be used as a revision aid.

The road to suicide (Page 21)
This page provides a summary of the off-stage events of the play that lead Eva to suicide. It will help clarify the events for which the Inspector holds the other characters responsible.

Headline news (Page 22)
This task involves students writing in a journalistic style about at least one of the main events of the play. It is important as an analytical exercise and as an exercise in using a particular style.

Characters

Birling, Mrs Birling, Sheila, Eric, Gerald, The Inspector (Pages 23–28)
These six sheets ask students to look at the main characters. They need to look for relevant evidence in terms of the character's speech and actions and the way he or she is responded to by others. Each exercise concludes with a character study.

Character evaluation and relationships

Labour conflict (Page 29)
In this activity, students consider the nature of labour conflicts and strikes. This then develops into a discussion that asks for quotations to support assertions about the attitudes of Arthur and Eric Birling to the strike.

Teachers' notes

The charity organisation (Page 30)
This sheet asks students to act out a situation in which someone is forced to justify a request for money. It then focuses on the specific issue of Sybil Birling's refusal to help Eva Smith.

Eric alone (Page 31)
This is an empathetic task that encourages a response to the situation in which Eric finds himself before his 'confession' to the Inspector.

The mysterious Inspector (Page 32)
Students are asked to look for evidence of the Inspector's dual role: as a regular policeman and as an omniscient judge. When they have done this, they are to complete a short writing task.

Seven deadly sins (Page 33)
This is a task that focuses on the hypocritical world views of Gerald and the Birlings. It does so by drawing attention to the way that all characters appear to have committed at least one of the seven deadly sins. Teachers should ensure students understand the meaning of each of the sins before starting Question 2.

The serving girl (Page 34)
This is an exercise involving empathy with Edna: it is designed to show that the Birlings' view of themselves may not be consistent with those others hold.

An exchange of letters (Page 35)
In this activity, students must think about the consequences of the Inspector's visit on Gerald and Sheila. The main point is for students to understand the possible influence the visit has had in terms of their future lives.

Eva's diary (Page 36)
As with **'The Road to Suicide'**, this sheet focuses on the events that take place before the play, the significance of which lies in their consequences. This time, however, the events are seen through the eyes of Eva herself.

The performance

Theatre programme (Page 37)
This sheet asks students to consider the play from the perspective of having to write a theatre programme. It should allow an examination of the play as both a commercial and an artistic product.

Setting the stage (Page 38)
Students are encouraged to think about the play in performance. The practical concerns of staging a play should be at the fore, and this sheet emphasises the function and importance of stage and set directions.

The audition (Page 39)
The tasks on this sheet allow for a consideration of the play in performance. Students should try as hard as possible to interpret the distinct personalities of the characters they are representing.

Essay practice

Answering essay questions, The first paragraph, Using quotations (Pages 40–42)
These sheets provide some general advice on how to approach the kinds of question asked at exam level, how to begin the essay and how to integrate quotations. Each provides a passage that demonstrates the type of response needed for particular writing tasks. Students can refer to these passages when writing their own responses.

How men are, Women's roles, Parents and children, Scandal! (Pages 43–46)
These sheets provide essay practice based on past exam and coursework questions. Sample passages are provided where appropriate so that students gain access to the style and content present in successful essays. The first two sheets consider the different roles assigned to men and women in the play. **'Parents and children'** encourages analysis of the relationships between the parents and children in the Birling family and **'Scandal!'** focuses on one of the play's main themes: hypocrisy. The aim of the sheets is to encourage confidence and fluency in analytical writing through a systematic approach to essay construction.

Exam passage

Exam passage (Page 47)
This exam passage follows the format used by some examination boards. It is relatively straightforward, and can be used as a basic text comprehension exercise.

Answers

Selected answers (Page 48)
This page gives solutions to **'Guess who?'** (Page 7), **'Who says?'** (Page 14), **'Crossword'** (Page 15) and **'The road to suicide'** (Page 21).

Predictions

FOCUS

- To think and talk about the possible outcomes *An Inspector Calls* may have.

1. You are about to begin studying *An Inspector Calls* by J B Priestley. Read this information about the play to get you started.

Themes
- Social class
- Power
- Injustice
- Guilt
- Responsibility

Some things that happen
- The Birlings and Gerald Croft are having a family celebration. Gerald and Sheila Birling become engaged.
- Inspector Goole arrives, announcing the death by suicide of a young woman called Eva Smith.
- The Inspector establishes that each of the characters has encountered Eva Smith in the past. One by one, he cross examines them about their part in her suicide.
- When the Inspector leaves the house, the family recognise he is not a real inspector at all.

The characters
- **Arthur Birling**: a pompous, man. He is the owner of a local factory and cares far more about profit than about the well-being of his workers.
- **Sybil Birling**: his wife. Very aware of her social position. She is a cold, unsympathetic woman, but she does a lot of work for charity.
- **Eric Birling**: their son. He is a weak and sometimes reckless young man with a drink problem. Unlike his parents, however, he does have a social conscience.
- **Sheila Birling**: their daughter. A vain and frivolous woman who is often very emotional. She suffers from jealousy at times, but does value honesty.
- **Gerald Croft**: the handsome son of a titled family. Confident with good manners.
- **Inspector Goole**: impressive, if rather mysterious. He wants all the characters to admit their part in Eva's death.
- **Eva Smith**: commits suicide. She is a pretty young woman, but ultimately penniless and alone in the world.

2. Working in pairs, discuss how you think the play might work out and what might happen. Consider:
   - how the characters might have had a direct or indirect part in Eva's death as the Inspector claims
   - who you think might admit their guilt and who might deny it
   - who or what the mysterious Inspector is
   - what 'message' or point J B Priestley might have wanted to make when he wrote the play.

Guess who?

FOCUS

- To identify the characters and their language.

1. Look at the portraits below. These are an artist's impression of each character. Study them carefully and think about what you know about each of them. Label each portrait with the name of the person it suits best.

a.

____

b.

____

c.

____

d.

____

e.

____

f.

____

2. Now, identify from the play who speaks the following words in each case.

   a. "As if a girl of that sort would ever refuse money!" Said by ______________________

   b. "This girl killed herself – and died a horrible death. But each of you helped to kill her. Remember that." Said by ______________________

   c. "And I'm talking as a hard-headed practical man of business." Said by ______________________

   d. "I've had a few drinks, ... and I've got a headache ..." Said by ______________________

   e. "You be careful – or I'll start weeping." Said by ______________________

   f. "In fact, I insist upon being one of the family now." Said by ______________________

Moral dilemmas

FOCUS

- To imagine yourself confronting the situations faced by the characters in *An Inspector Calls*.

- Look at the following dilemmas. Read each of them and write answers to the questions that follow.

a. You are a young man from a wealthy family engaged to a woman you like a lot. Her parents are also wealthy, and your marriage would leave you financially secure for the rest of your life. One night, however, you meet a girl in a bar: you immediately find her attractive. You talk and agree to meet her again. Your feelings for each other intensify. There is a problem, though: she has no money, no job, and it is very likely that you will be rejected by your own family if your relationship becomes public.
What will you do and why?

b. You are a successful businessman and own a factory employing mainly young women. You do not pay them very much, but they do their jobs well. One day, they go on strike, asking for a small pay increase you know you could afford to pay. You also know that the strikers do not have much money in reserve and probably will not last out for much longer than two weeks. The strike is being led by about five of your best workers.
How do you deal with the strike?

c. You go to your favourite dress shop where your mother is one of the most valued customers. You try a dress on that looks awful on you. When you look in the mirror, you see a pretty shop assistant laughing: you think she is laughing at you.
How do you react?

d. You are the most important member of a women's charity organisation that offers financial help to people in trouble. One day a girl comes to you. When you ask her name, she uses your own quite unusual family name and, when you become offended, changes it to something else. She tells you she is pregnant by her husband who has now left her. She then admits, after some questioning, that she is not married. Finally, she says that the man responsible offered her money, but she refused it, believing it was stolen.
Do you think the girl should be given financial help by the charity organisation?

Reading a play

FOCUS

- To understand the differences between a play and a novel through rewriting part of the play in prose.

Introduction

A play depends almost entirely on dialogue between characters to tell its story and uses only the briefest of descriptions either to set the scene or to give stage directions. This is because a play is not meant simply to be read but to be performed on stage. It is the job of the director of the play and the actors and actresses to interpret how it should be performed.

1. Look at the opening of Act 1 and read down to:

> **EDNA** [*going*] Yes, ma'am.
> [EDNA *goes out. They now have all the glasses filled.*
> BIRLING *beams at them and clearly relaxes.*]

If this was the opening of a novel, we would be given much more information than we are given here, such as:

- extra details about what the characters look like, how they behave, their thoughts and feelings
- more details about their surroundings, the atmosphere in the room and so on.

When we read a play, however, we have to rely quite heavily on our imaginations and create for ourselves a picture of what the scene would really be like.

2. To give you a better sense of the differences described here, try rewriting what you have just read as if it were the opening of a novel. Use some of the speech from the play if you wish. You could start like this:

Arthur Birling sat back in his chair and considered the delicious dinner already being digested in the depths of his rather portly belly. A hint of a smile curled the edges of his lips as he surveyed with satisfaction the family gathering before him. "Giving us the port, Edna? That's right," he said, in an unusually jolly sort of way. With chubby fingers, he pushed a crystal decanter towards his son, Eric. The evening was still young and tonight he was feeling pleased, very pleased indeed.

3. When you have finished, you will find that you have had to use your imagination to fill in the gaps left by the playscript. This is also what you will need to do in your own mind as you are reading the rest of *An Inspector Calls*.

The Inspector's notebook I

FOCUS

- To take the role of the Inspector and make notes on Eva Smith, Arthur Birling and Sheila Birling.

- Using the sections from the Inspector's notebook below, fill in the information he finds out about Eva's suicide as the investigation proceeds. Include information about how the named characters respond to his accusations.

Eva Smith (alias Daisy Renton)

Committed suicide in a horrible way.

Arthur Birling

Eva's former employer. She worked in the Birling factory two years ago.

Sheila Birling

Met Eva at Milwards dress shop where she worked as an assistant.

The Inspector's notebook 2

FOCUS

- To take the role of the Inspector and make notes on Gerald Croft, Sybil Birling and Eric Birling.

- Using the sections from the Inspector's notebook below, fill in the information he finds out about Eva's suicide as the investigation proceeds. Include information about how the named characters respond to his accusations.

Gerald Croft

Came across Eva for the first time in March last year in the stalls bar at the Palace.

Sybil Birling

Two weeks ago she used her position as a prominent member of a charity organisation to reject Eva's request for help.

Eric Birling

Was 'squiffy' in the stalls bar at the Palace when he met Eva one night last November.

A golden age

FOCUS

- To research the social and historical background to *An Inspector Calls.*

1. Read the following.

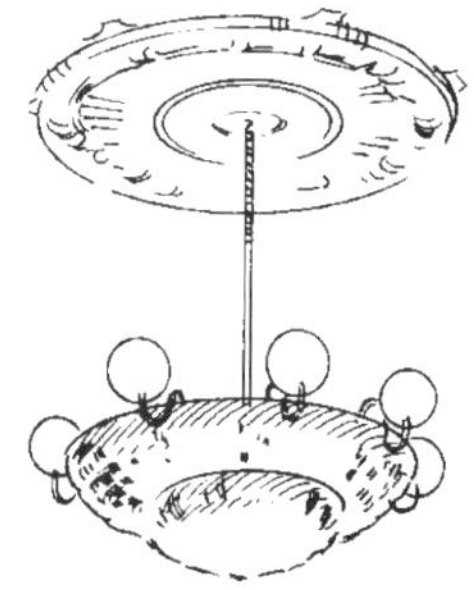

The time from Queen Victoria's death in 1901 to the outbreak of the First World War in 1914 was often referred to at the time, and by some historians since, as a 'golden age'. For certain people – the wealthy upper and middle classes – this was true. The strict Victorian Age was swept away and the rich were able to enjoy a life of great comfort and leisure. They had servants at home who did all the housework and cooking for them, and with so much money and time on their hands they were able to enjoy a wide variety of entertainments: dinner parties, dances, opera, the theatre, holidays at the seaside; and some of the social events of the year, such as racing at Ascot, or yachting at Cowes. For the working classes, things also began to improve. In 1906, the Compensation Act was passed, which forced employers to compensate injured workmen; in 1908, Old Age Pensions were introduced; and in 1911, National Insurance was set up to provide workers with sickness benefit and basic medical care. However, the conditions in factories and industry were still very poor. The hours were long, the wages were low, and the workers were often badly treated by their employers. Furthermore, they were forced to live in cramped and uncomfortable housing and, without much money, large families were frequently reduced to living in one room with little by way of comfort.

2. Was this really, then, a golden age? Use your school library – or other sources – to find out more about the lives of the rich, the poor and particularly women during this period. This information will help you with the task below.

3. Now think back to *An Inspector Calls.* Working in pairs, choose either to write about Eva or Sheila.

   Using what you know about the woman you have chosen, whether it is Sheila with her wealth and life of leisure, or Eva with her more difficult, poorer life, write an account of a typical day in their lives. Try to use what you have found out during your research. The day you describe should take place when Eva is still working at the Birling factory and the two young women have not yet met.

4. When you have finished, swap your work with a partner and find out how different his/her account is.

The future

FOCUS

- To understand and use dramatic irony.

Introduction

Birling's optimistic speech about the bright future the young people face is a key point in Act 1. Birling tells Gerald and Sheila they are marrying at a 'very good time'. However, the play is set in 1912, and was first performed in 1946. Audiences would have known that Birling's predictions are wrong, because they would realise that 1912 was certainly not a good time to be marrying; after all, the First World War began only two years later. This technique of allowing the audience to know more than the characters in a play is called **dramatic irony**. It is often used to draw attention to how wrong a character's beliefs or opinions are.

1. Read the section in Act 1 where Birling says, "I'm delighted about this engagement ..." down to "... Russia, which will always be behindhand, naturally." Note down the parts of his speeches that history proved wrong.

2. We live in a similar time to Arthur Birling. Although there are worries about the future; progress in technology and the fact that there has not been a world war for over 50 years have given most people in Britain a reasonably optimistic outlook. But then, we may be very wrong. In pairs, write down a list of things that worry people nowadays about the future. Try to be as specific as you can.

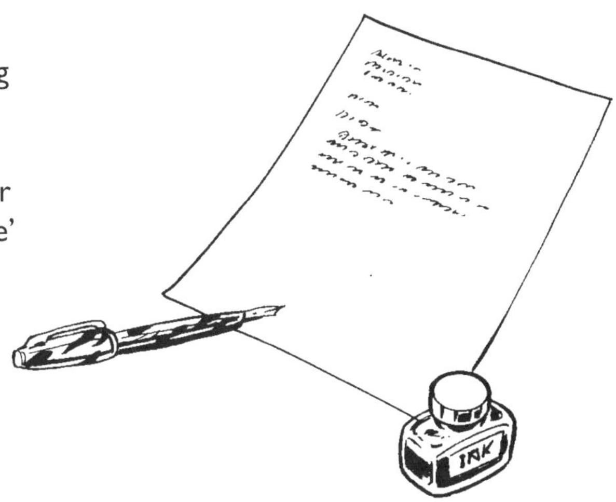

3. Now, imagine you are a middle-aged person called Birling in a modern-day setting equivalent to Arthur Birling's situation in 1912. Write a letter to a young man and woman you know (such as a son or daughter and his/her fiancé(e)) to convince them that now is a 'very good time' to get married. Choose three or four of the anxieties from your earlier list and try to persuade the young people that they are not worth worrying about. Use Birling's style as much as possible.

   Here is an example to get you started.

> And let me tell you both this. You may well have heard from a load of 'new age travellers' or whatever they call themselves, that life on earth is about to come to an end just because we cut down a few trees in the rainforest. They don't know what they're talking about. Most of them have never done a day's work in their lives. They just lie around all day listening to their music, or what they call music: it sounds like a load of cats wailing to me ...

Who says?

FOCUS

- To think about and revise what the main characters in the play reveal about themselves through their speech.

1. Look at the list of quotations below. Each of the quotations is taken from either Act 1 or Act 2. As you are reading, use your judgement and a copy of the text if necessary to write down who says what.

a. "But after all it's better to ask for the earth than to take it."

Said by________________

b. "You'd think a girl had never had any clothes before she gets married. Women are potty about 'em."

Said by________________

c. "... it would do us all a bit of good if sometimes we tried to put ourselves in the place of the young women counting their pennies in their dingy little back bedrooms."

Said by________________

d. "I hate those hard-eyed dough-faced women."

Said by________________

e. "We were having a nice little family celebration tonight. And a nasty mess you've made of it now, haven't you?"

Said by________________

f. "But these girls aren't cheap labour – they're people."

Said by________________

g. "You're looking tired, dear. I think you ought to go to bed – and forget about this absurd business."

Said by________________

h. "You mustn't try to build up a kind of wall between us and that girl. If you do, then the Inspector will just break it down."

Said by________________

2. Now, go through Act 3. Choose five quotations that are typical of the people who have said them. Test other members of your class to find out if they can identify each individual speaker.

Crossword

FOCUS

- To test your knowledge of *An Inspector Calls*.

- Complete this crossword.

Across

1 Gerald gives this to Sheila. (10, 4)
7 An 'icy' word to describe Mrs Birling. (4)
8 The Inspector has an air of this about him. (7)
9 Strangely, it sounds like 'ghoul'. (5)
10 The Birlings are no longer a happy one. (6)
12 Eric is too fond of this. (5)
14 'We know, but the characters do not.' (8, 5)
16 Eric feels this as the truth comes out. (4)
17 The German leader Birling does not rate. (6)
21 The ship so admired by Birling. (7)
22 Eva kept one, and the Inspector uses it. (5)
25 The Inspector's arrival interrupts it. (5)
26 One of Eva's aliases. (5)
27 Edna's position. (4)

Down

2 It's not the Inspector's game! (4)
3 The public position held by Birling two years ago. (5)
4 Eva frequently changes hers. (4)
5 The Inspector wants the other characters to take it. (14)
6 Sheila loves him at the beginning of the play. (6)
7 Birling's business competitors. (6)
11 Apparently Eva was a good one during the strike. (6)
12 Mr and Mrs Birling both claim to have done theirs. (4)
13 Something that Eva needs. (5)
15 Mrs Birling is guilty of this. (5)
18 *An Inspector Calls* is an example. (5)
19 Eric does this in desperation. (5)
20 Mr Birling's sin. (5)
23 Sheila's answer when Gerald first proposes. (3)
24 The tragic heroine. (3)

Pre-twentieth century: 'Everyman'

FOCUS

- To familiarise yourself with the striking parallels between *An Inspector Calls* and *Everyman*.

Introduction

The idea of a supernatural, or at the very least a mysterious figure, visiting mankind to confront him with his sins is not a new one in literature.

- Read the following extract.

In the nineteenth century, Dickens did something very similar to J B Priestley when Marley's ghost in *A Christmas Carol* persuades Scrooge to cast off his wicked ways. Shakespeare, too, used ghosts and spirits to chastise evildoers, for example in *Macbeth*. It was in the Morality Plays written and performed in the fifteenth century that this idea was at its most popular. The most famous of these is called *Everyman*.

The story of *Everyman* begins when God, angered by the greed and sinfulness of mankind, sends his messenger, Death, to show a typical person, or Everyman, why his selfishness and worldly pleasures will lead him to eternal damnation. It is Death's job to demonstrate that good deeds rather than vice form the road to Heaven. At the end of the play, therefore, Everyman is able to see the error of his ways and, by repenting of his sins, is saved from the fires of hell.

- Read Extract 1, taken from the beginning of *Everyman*. In it, God is considering what to do now that so many people have drifted away from Him into a life of sin.

Extract 1

GOD I perceive, here in my majesty,
How that all creatures be to me unkind,
Living without dread in worldly prosperity,
Of holy sight the people be so blind,
Drowned in sin, they know me not for their God:
In worldly riches is all their mind …
… And now I see the people do clean forsake me.
They use the seven deadly sins damnable;
As pride, covetise, wrath and lechery,
Now in the world be made commendable:
And thus they leave of angels the heavenly company …
Therefore I will, in all the haste,
Have a reckoning of Everyman's person;
For, if I leave the people thus alone
In their life and wicked tempests,
Verily they will become much worse than beasts:
For now one would by envy another up eat;
Charity they all do clean forget.

Pre-twentieth century: 'Everyman' (continued)

FOCUS

- To familiarise yourself with the text of *Everyman* and the striking parallels between *An Inspector Calls* and *Everyman*.

- Extract 2 is taken from the end of the play, *Everyman*, and is spoken by a doctor who has witnessed Everyman repenting his past behaviour and praising God. Read the extract.

Extract 2

DOCTOR … And he that hath his account whole and sound,
High in heaven he shall be crowned;
Unto which place God bring us all thither,
That we may live body and soul together.
There to help the trinity!
Amen say ye, for saint charity.

- Now, answer the following questions.

1. What similarities can you see in the roles played by Death (as mentioned in the introduction) and Inspector Goole?
2. In what ways are the sins mentioned in the first extract similar to those committed by Gerald and the Birling family?
3. At the end of *Everyman*, the central character is saved. Can the same be said for the characters in *An Inspector Calls*?
4. Look at the words in the second extract that read: "That we may live body and soul together". Now look at the Inspector's final speech given below. Can you find a similar idea in it?

INSPECTOR

But just remember this. One Eva Smith has gone – but there are millions and millions and millions of Eva Smiths and John Smiths still left with us, with their lives, their hopes and fears, their suffering, and chance of happiness, all intertwined with our lives, with what we think and say and do. We don't live alone. We are members of one body. We are responsible for each other. And I tell you that the time will soon come when, if men will not learn that lesson, then they will be taught it in fire and blood and anguish. Good night.

5. What is the link between the idea of Everyman and the name Eva Smith?
6. Look at the Inspector's warning that "… if men will not learn that lesson, then they will be taught it in fire and blood and anguish". What is the connection between this message and the message in *Everyman*?

Key episodes: Act 1

FOCUS

- To revise the key episodes of Act 1.

1. Look at the pictures and captions below. Study them carefully and then answer the questions that follow. You will need to refer to the play.

a. Gerald gives Sheila an engagement ring.

b. Birling makes a speech about future progress.

c. Birling tells Gerald that he may be getting a knighthood.

d. The Inspector calls and the mood changes immediately.

e. Birling denies all responsibility for Eva's death.

f. Birling and Eric argue about the strike and Eva's treatment.

g. Sheila is upset by the news of Eva's death and admits her guilt.

h. Sheila confronts Gerald about his relationship with Eva.

2. Look at boxes **a** and **h**. How has the relationship between Gerald and Sheila changed?
3. Look at boxes **b**, **c**, **e** and **f**. What do these episodes tell us about Birling's character?
4. Look at boxes **c** and **d**. Why is Birling so keen to tell Gerald about the possibility of his knighthood? What difference does the Inspector's visit make to this?
5. Look at box **d**. What is it about the way the Inspector speaks and behaves that makes him at once such an impressive character?
6. Look at box **f**. What do we learn about the differences between father and son at this point?
7. Look at boxes **g** and **h**. What qualities are there to admire in Sheila's behaviour at these times?

Key episodes: Act 2

FOCUS

- To revise the key episodes of Act 2.

1. Look at the pictures and captions below. Study them carefully and then answer the questions that follow. You will need to refer to the play.

a. Sheila refuses to leave the room during Gerald's confession.

b. Mrs Birling arrives and greets the Inspector with cold politeness.

c. Mrs Birling is astonished to find that Eric drinks too much.

d. Gerald becomes upset as he begins the story of meeting Eva.

e. Sheila returns the engagement ring to Gerald who then leaves.

f. Mrs Birling says she does not recognise the photograph of Eva.

g. Mrs Birling flatly denies responsibility for Eva's death.

h. Mrs Birling finds to her horror that Eric made Eva pregnant.

2. Look at boxes **a** and **e**. How has Sheila's opinion of Gerald's behaviour changed between the boxes?
3. Look at box **b**. How is Mrs Birling's reaction to the Inspector's visit different from the other characters' reactions?
4. Look at box **d**. Do you think Gerald is genuinely upset. Consider his behaviour both before and after?
5. Look at boxes **c** and **h**. What do these moments teach us about the relationship between Sybil Birling and her son?
6. Look at boxes **f** and **g**. How do Sybil Birling's responses to enquiries about Eva Smith compare with her husband's?
7. Look at box **h**. Priestley ends this and each of the other acts in a very startling way. What effect does this have?

Key episodes: Act 3

FOCUS

- To revise the key episodes of Act 3.

1. Look at the pictures and captions below. Study them carefully and then answer the questions that follow. You will need to refer to the play.

a. All the Birlings are in conflict and Eric needs a drink.

b. Eric admits he stole money from the family business.

c. Eric blames his mother for Eva's suicide.

d. The Inspector warns they must accept their guilt, and then leaves.

e. Gerald returns and the family concludes the Inspector was not 'real'.

f. All are cheerful except for Sheila and Eric.

g. Sheila refuses to take back Gerald's engagement ring.

h. A phone call confirms that a girl has died after swallowing disinfectant.

2. Look at boxes **a** and **f**. How has the mood in the dining room changed between these two points?
3. Look at boxes **a**, **b** and **c**. What do these episodes reveal about Eric's character and behaviour?
4. Look at box **d**. Which characters do you think are the most affected by what the Inspector says?
5. Look at boxes **e** and **f**. Why are Gerald, Birling and Mrs Birling so pleased to find that Goole was not a policeman?
6. Look at box **g**. Why does Sheila refuse to take back Gerald's engagement ring?
7. Look at box **h**. What does this information suggest about Inspector Goole?

The road to suicide

FOCUS

- To understand the events for which the Inspector holds the characters responsible.

- The pictures below portray important moments in the events leading up to Eva Smith's suicide. Cut out the pictures, arrange them in the correct order and stick them on to a piece of paper. Find quotations that show how each of the characters feel as they look back on their involvement with Eva and write each quotation beneath the appropriate picture.

Eva meets Gerald at the Palace bar and they get to know each other.

Eva meets Eric at the Palace bar. He is drunk and insists on taking her back to her flat. Soon they begin an affair.

Sheila tries on a dress at Milwards and is furious when she sees Eva apparently mocking her. Sheila threatens to close the Birling account if Eva is not sacked.

Hopeless and destitute, Eva commits suicide. She swallows a strong bottle of disinfectant that burns her insides.

Eva is one of the leaders in a strike at Birling's factory. She protests against low wages. All ringleaders, including Eva, are sacked.

Gerald gives Eva (Daisy) money and a place to stay. She falls in love with him, but after a while he breaks off the relationship.

Eva goes to the seaside for two months. She wants to be alone to remember the happy times she has had with Gerald.

Eva tells Eric that she is pregnant but will not marry him. He gives her money, but she refuses to accept it: she suspects it is stolen.

Calling herself Mrs Birling, Eva appeals to the Brumley Women's Charity Organisation for help. Mrs Birling rejects her appeal.

Headline news

FOCUS

- To write in a journalistic style about one of the main events in the play.

1. Look at the newspaper headlines below, and identify the section(s) in the play to which each refers.

2. Choose one of the headlines and write a newspaper report. Here are some guidelines and ideas to help you.

   - Newspaper articles are written in columns.
   - Paragraphs are short and to the point: the first paragraph must give the who, what, where, when and, if possible, why.
   - Focus on the particular storyline you want to report on. You may need to give some background details but these should be stated briefly. Do not retell the whole of *An Inspector Calls*.
   - Eyewitnesses are often quoted in newspaper reports: use both direct and indirect speech.
   - You could use pictures and captions for extra interest.

Birling

FOCUS

- To make a character study of Birling.

1. To make the fullest possible study of a character we need to look at what he/she is like and how other people respond to him/her. Record your ideas about Birling under the headings provided.

What he says

What others say about him

What he thinks

What others think about him

How he behaves

How others behave towards him

2. When you have completed your notes, use the back of this sheet to record any further quotations or evidence to support your ideas.

3. Now, write a character study of Birling.

Mrs Birling

FOCUS

- To make a character study of Mrs Birling.

1. To make the fullest possible study of a character we need to look at what he/she is like and how other people respond to him/her. Record your ideas about Mrs Birling under the headings provided.

What she says

What others say about her

What she thinks

What others think about her

How she behaves

How others behave towards her

2. When you have completed your notes, use the back of this sheet to record any further quotations or evidence to support your ideas.

3. Now write a character study of Mrs Birling.

Sheila

FOCUS

- To make a character study of Sheila.

1. To make the fullest possible study of a character we need to look at what he/she is like and how other people respond to him/her. Record your ideas about Sheila under the headings provided.

What she says

What others say about her

What she thinks

What others think about her

How she behaves

How others behave towards her

2. When you have completed your notes, use the back of this sheet to record any further quotations or evidence to support your ideas.

3. Now write a character study of Sheila.

Eric

FOCUS

- To make a character study of Eric.

1. To make the fullest possible study of a character we need to look at what he/she is like and how other people respond to him/her. Record your ideas about Eric under the headings provided.

What he says

What others say about him

What he thinks

What others think about him

How he behaves

How others behave towards him

2. When you have completed your notes, use the back of this sheet to record any further quotations or evidence to support your ideas.

3. Now write a character study of Eric.

Gerald

FOCUS

- To make a character study of Gerald.

1. To make the fullest possible study of a character we need to look at what he/she is like and how other people respond to him/her. Record your ideas about Gerald under the headings provided.

What he says

What others say about him

What he thinks

What others think about him

How he behaves

How others behave towards him

2. When you have completed your notes, use the back of this sheet to record any further quotations or evidence to support your ideas.

3. Now write a character study of Gerald.

The Inspector

FOCUS

- To make a character study of the Inspector.

1. To make the fullest possible study of a character we need to look at what he/she is like and how other people respond to him/her. Record your ideas about the Inspector under the headings provided.

What he says

What others say about him

What he thinks

What others think about him

How he behaves

How others behave towards him

2. When you have completed your notes, use the back of this sheet to record any further quotations or evidence to support your ideas.

3. Now write a character study of the Inspector.

Labour conflict

FOCUS

- To consider the nature of labour conflict.

1. Eva is sacked by Birling for being a leader of a strike in his factory. As a class, discuss what you know about strikes. You should consider:
   - why workers sometimes strike
   - any famous strikes you have heard of
   - why some strikes are successful while others fail.

2. Now, read the passage in Act I beginning just after the Inspector has shown Birling Eva Smith's photograph.

It starts:	**INSPECTOR**	I think you remember Eva Smith now, don't you, Mr Birling?
And ends:	**BIRLING**	Yes. The girl had been causing trouble in the works. I was quite justified.

3. Using the questions below for guidance, what evidence can you find that Birling and Eric are in conflict over Birling's handling of the strike in which Eva was sacked?

   Find quotations from the passage you have just read for each question. If necessary, add words to the quotations for them to make sense. Remember that if you need to use your own words, you should put them in brackets. If necessary, cut long quotations down using ellipses (dots to show words you have left out). Try not to use quotations of more than **ten words**. Set your quotations out as in the example below.

   a. What is Birling's attitude towards Eva's death?

      "... there's nothing mysterious – or scandalous – about this business ..."
      "(The sacking) has nothing whatever to do with the ... suicide."

   b. What did Birling think about Eva's ability as a worker?
   c. Why did Birling refuse the workers' demands for a pay increase?
   d. What does Eric think about Eva and the strikers?

The charity organisation

FOCUS

- To understand Eva's situation better through acting out a situation in which someone is forced to justify a request for money.

1. Read the following passage.

At the time in which *An Inspector Calls* was set, there was no social security provided by the government. This meant that people who fell on hard times would have to fend for themselves, turn to their families, or seek charity. Around the country there were many charities set up for this purpose by the wealthy wives of businessmen and professionals. Some of them did a great deal of good and were extremely well run. Many of them, however, were organised by people with no real interest or knowledge of the lives lived by those they were supposed to be helping. The poor would often have to prove, in a humiliating interview, that they were worthy applicants. Often a request for help would be turned down because the applicant was judged for some reason not to deserve it.

2. Get into groups of three or four in order to act out a scene in which a man or woman is forced to go before a charity committee to ask for help.

   Remember that the person asking for assistance will have to have some very good reasons for doing so. They have to prove they are desperately poor and are not to blame for their own poverty. They will have to assure the committee that their character is good, and that if any help is given they will not waste it.

   Write down three reasons for the person's poverty.

   Plan how such a scene would work and then act it out. A good scene will emphasise the enormous difference in power between the person asking for help and those who are able to give it.

3. By refusing to give Eva Smith help when she goes before the committee, Mrs Birling plays an important part in Eva's decision to commit suicide. We only know about the interview, however, because the Inspector questions Mrs Birling about it. It actually takes place two weeks before the action of the play.

   Write down the script of the interview that might have taken place between Eva Smith and Mrs Birling's committee. Try to convey a sense of Eva's desperation and the superior attitude the committee would show her.

Eric alone

FOCUS

- To investigate what might be going on off-stage to shed light on the main action.

Introduction
Whilst Mrs Birling is being interviewed by the Inspector in Act 2, we hear the front door slam. Arthur Birling soon finds out that the noise has been caused by Eric leaving the house. At this point, Eric is aware of his part in Eva Smith's death and he wants some time alone, away from the others to collect his thoughts.

1. Your task is to write down the thoughts going through Eric's mind during the ten minutes when he is outside the house, pacing the street. First, read from the beginning of Act 3 down to:

   ERIC My God – I'm not likely to forget.

   Reading this section will help make clear in your own mind exactly what Eric has done.

2. Now, make brief notes about the following.

a. **What Eric feels about Eva, especially now she is dead.**	b. **Eric's emotions concerning Eva's pregnancy.**
c. **The fears Eric may have about his theft becoming public.**	d. **Eric's thoughts about the other members of his family.**

3. Now, write the account of Eric's thoughts, in the first person, as if you are Eric.

The mysterious Inspector

FOCUS

- To understand more about the character and nature of the Inspector.

Introduction

In some ways, Inspector Goole is like a regular policeman. In other ways he is much more than that. He knows far more than an ordinary inspector could possibly know and his prediction about Eva Smith's death certainly has something supernatural about it. Even the name, Goole, sounds like 'ghoul'.

1. Get into groups of three or six. One or two people should be responsible for finding examples of the way Inspector Goole behaves in each act of the play. Make a list of occasions when he is behaving normally, and a list of occasions when his conduct is odd. Complete the table below.

Normal for an inspector	Odd for an inspector
– Dressed in a plain dark suit. – Shows Birling photographic evidence.	– Interrupts Birling rudely. – Stops others seeing photograph.

2. Share your findings with the rest of your group.

3. Now, write three short paragraphs in answer to the questions below. Use the information you have found to help you.

a. In what ways can the Inspector be seen as just an ordinary policeman?
b. Describe how the Inspector is shown to be a mystery.
c. Why do you think Priestley wanted the Inspector to be both ordinary and mysterious?

Seven deadly sins

FOCUS

- To identify the seven sins that the Birlings and Gerald Croft commit between them.

Introduction

In *An Inspector Calls*, Priestley explores the way that evil may be committed by people who would probably consider themselves perfect Christians. The Birlings and Gerald Croft believe that they are all good at the beginning of the play, but all commit at least one of the seven deadly sins.

Here is a list of the seven deadly sins.

pride wrath envy lust gluttony avarice sloth

1. Some of these words may be unfamiliar to you. Use a dictionary and a thesaurus to find out their precise meanings. For each of the seven words, write an exact definition and a set of alternative words that have the same or similar meanings.

2. Throughout the play, Priestley wants his audiences to understand that the Birlings and Gerald Croft are not such perfect people as they seem. Indeed, to 'keep up appearances', they lie to each other, to people outside their family and, most of all, to themselves. As the play begins, they have convinced themselves of their own goodness. The Inspector is there to open their eyes.

   Next to the following names write the sin or sins you think each commits.
   Then on a separate piece of paper, write evidence that supports each of your ideas.

Birling ______________________________

Mrs Birling ______________________________

Eric ______________________________

Sheila ______________________________

Gerald ______________________________

3. Other character faults we often talk about are hypocrisy (being 'two-faced') and snobbery (looking down on people and their behaviour in the belief that you are superior). Write an account explaining which characters are guilty of hypocrisy and snobbery and in what ways.

The serving girl

FOCUS

- To look at the events through the eyes of Edna to obtain an outside view of the Birlings.

Introduction

The Birlings, by and large, see themselves as decent, important and respected members of the community. They are viewed, however, somewhat differently by others outside their circle.

- Imagine you are Edna and write, in the form of a diary, your impressions of the Birlings and of Gerald Croft. Remember that Edna's style of writing is likely to be different from that of the Birlings. It would probably be chatty and informal. Her description of Eric Birling is started for you. Try to use a similar style for the others.

Dear Diary

Another hard day scrubbing floors and cooking for the Birlings. They work me like a slave and pay me almost nothing. They make themselves out to be so perfect you'd think butter wouldn't melt in their mouths. But they're not. Look at that son of theirs, Eric. He must be the same age as me and I bet he's never done a day's work in his life. All he does is lounge around all day. He goes to the factory sometimes with his dad but some of the girls tell me he don't do nothing when he's there. Well, maybe 'nothing' isn't the right way of putting it. What he doesn't do in his office he makes up for in hanging around the machines where the girls work. Some of the things they say he's said to them are shameful. And the drinking! Mrs Birling don't know about it, but I've heard him come home in the middle of the night as drunk as a lord ...

An exchange of letters

FOCUS

- To think about the consequences of the Inspector's call through the eyes of Gerald and Sheila.

- Imagine two weeks have passed since the Inspector's visit. Gerald and Sheila have neither seen nor spoken to each other in this time. Anxious to resume their relationship, Gerald writes a letter to Sheila trying to convince her that things can still be as they were before. Having received the letter, Sheila writes back with her reply.

- Write the two letters using the notes below to help you.

Gerald's letter: points to consider

- Gerald is likely to take a persuasive tone: he will want to remind Sheila of all the happy times they have had together: invent these if you want to, since they are not mentioned in the play.
- He will apologise passionately for his affair with Eva Smith and will promise faithfully that nothing like this will ever happen again.
- He will mention the Inspector's visit, but will probably concentrate on the fact that nothing will come of it.
- Gerald will probably finish the letter by declaring his love for Sheila and begging her to come back.

Sheila's letter: points to consider

- Sheila may write back with politeness and understanding: do not forget that even though Gerald has been unfaithful to her, she says she respects him more than she has "ever done before", probably because he finally tells the truth and, amongst those who knew Eva, Gerald at least showed her some love and care.
- Sheila is changed more than anyone else by the experience of the Inspector's visit: she develops a far greater sense of responsibility and awareness.

Finally

- You will have to decide whether Sheila will accept Gerald back. There is no right or wrong answer to this, but you should remember that if you make Gerald write in a way that suggests his attitudes to life are unchanged (look again at what Gerald says at the end of the play), Sheila will be very unlikely to want to marry him. If, on the other hand, Gerald indicates that he too has been affected by what the Inspector said, Sheila will be far more likely to take him seriously.

Eva's diary

FOCUS

- To empathise with Eva through writing part of her diary.

Introduction
We find out about Eva Smith through other people and their descriptions of the meetings they have had with her, but we do not know about her personal thoughts and feelings. One way we can begin to understand Eva is to imagine her writing a diary of her experiences.

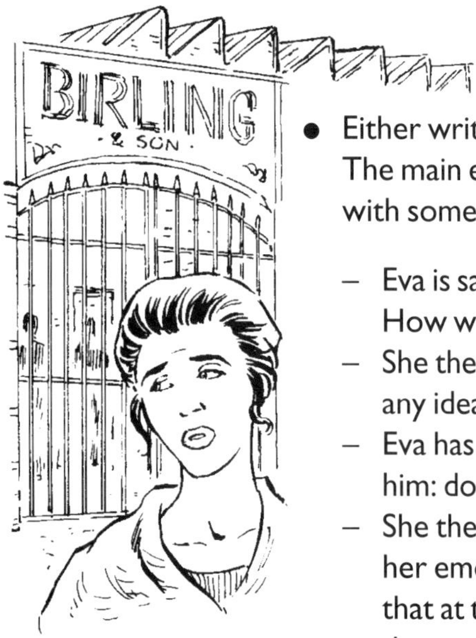

- Either write Eva's diary or choose one part of it to write in detail. The main events in Eva's sad decline are given below, together with some questions for you to think about.
  - Eva is sacked from Birling's factory after leading a strike. How would she feel about losing her job?
  - She then loses her job at Milwards. Do you think she has any idea of the reasons this happens?
  - Eva has a relationship with Gerald. What does she think of him: does she care about him?
  - She then has a relationship with Eric. What do you think her emotional responses to him would be? Do not forget that at this stage she is becoming more and more desperate.
  - The final straw for Eva is the refusal of Mrs Birling to help her. How would she feel as she leaves the committee with nothing to live on?

Below is an example of the way you could start the entry about Eva losing her job. You do not need to worry about dates, but do try to write in the same style as the example.

I've been sacked from the factory for doing what I thought was right. We work day in, day out for twenty-two and six. After rent and food that leaves none of us with anything to live on. I don't want to be rich and I've never been a greedy person, but I haven't saved a penny since I've worked for Birling and I can only go out once a month. The holiday I've just had with the other girls has used up everything I have. We all wanted twenty-five shillings a week and I was one of those prepared to stand up and say what I thought was right. It doesn't seem much to ask for and I know Birling can afford it.

Theatre programme

FOCUS

- To produce a theatre programme.

- Produce your own theatre programme for *An Inspector Calls*. Include the following elements.

1. A front cover

Write the title of the play and the name of the author clearly and boldly. You should also create a design or picture that is both striking and also hints at what the play is all about. For instance, you might focus on a theme such as greed, or poverty or injustice, or it might portray a character such as the Inspector or Eva Smith. Whatever you choose, remember that your main aim is to grab the attention of the public as effectively as you can.

2. J B Priestley's life and works

Write a very brief account of Priestley's life and works that includes things such as when and where he was born, his early life, his experiences and accomplishments, the kinds of things he wrote about, his greatest works and so on.

3. An introduction to the play

Your task here is to give the readers a taste of what the play is all about; to give them some background information and to encourage their interest in the performance itself. You might, for instance, give some idea of what England was like at the time in which the play is set and then link this with some of the themes and ideas that are explored through the drama itself. You could also mention some of the characters and what they are like. Do not write a summary of the whole play as you do not want to spoil the suspense.

4. A cast of actors

Choose a suitable cast of actors taken from famous films and television programmes to play the various roles in *An Inspector Calls*. If you wish, you can cut out pictures of the actors from magazines and stick them on to the page.

5. Quotations

Choose a quotation from each of the characters that tells us something important about the kind of people they are. Arrange the quotations in an interesting way on one of the pages.

6. Extracts from reviews

Invent a few lines from two or three critics who have written very positive reviews of the play for local newspapers and add these to your programme.

Setting the stage

FOCUS

- To look at the function and importance of stage and set directions in a playscript.

1. Read carefully through the information given by J B Priestley at the beginning of Act 1 about how the set and characters should look.

2. Here is one statement about the room from these directions.

   'The general effect is substantial and heavily comfortable, but not cosy and homelike.'

   Although this is a description of a room, it might equally have been a description of one of the characters. Which one and why?

3. Later, there is a description of the lighting that should be used. In pairs, find it, and then note down what key difference there is between the lighting used *before* the Inspector arrives and the lighting used *after*. Discuss why the author has suggested this.

4. Descriptions of the main characters and what they are doing follow. On your own, list the items that Edna, the maid, removes from the table, and what she replaces them with, including those items that remain.

   Write about 50 words explaining what some (if not all) of these items suggest about the Birlings way of life.

5. Now, reread the descriptions of the characters very carefully. In your own words, trying not to think about what you know happens later in the play, describe what overall impression is given of the family and their environment when the curtain rises. Include quotations to support your impression. You might wish to use some adjectives (where appropriate) from this list:

   rich   self-satisfied   proud   pleasant

   happy   comfortable   united

   important   welcoming   wealthy   relaxed

   attractive   cold   ostentatious

6. Finally, imagine that Eva moves to temporary lodgings before she becomes so desperate that she kills herself. Imagine that Eric is about to visit her. It is likely to be one room, as she has moved out of the 'nice little set of rooms' Gerald kept her in. Write your own description of the room/stage-set. It should reflect Eva's state of mind as she waits for Eric to call – remember that she has lost her job, is probably about to lose the room, and has little, if any, money.

The audition

FOCUS

- To perform part of the play to increase your understanding of the personalities of the characters and of the play in performance.

Introduction

The most important ingredient in the production of any play is the cast of actors. It is their responsibility to have a complete understanding of the characters they will portray on stage and they must use all their expertise to project those personalities to an audience. If they can do this effectively, it is likely that the whole production will be a success.

1. Get into groups of five or six. Imagine that each of you is auditioning for a part in *An Inspector Calls*. The director of the play has given you three sections to perform, each chosen because the mood of the characters and the atmosphere alters. It will be a measure of your skills to see how well you can show this. The sections are:

– The beginning of Act 1 to	**MRS BIRLING**	Now stop it, you two …
– The beginning of Act 2 to	**INSPECTOR**	You see, we have to share something ...
– The beginning of Act 3 to	**BIRLING**	You heard what I said.

Read through these sections carefully and then allocate roles to each member of your group, making sure that everybody has a roughly equal part to play overall. Remember, you need not learn all your lines for this. At an audition you can refer to a script but you would be expected to know your words well enough so that you only need glance at the page every now and again. What the director will be looking for, however, is for you to speak and act in a natural and convincing way as though you really are the character you are portraying.

2. Now, rehearse thoroughly.

3. Perform your three sections.

4. When all the groups have performed, your teacher, in the role of director, will choose the six successful actors who have won a part in the play. He or she will explain why those people have been chosen and which part they would be given in the actual production (it may, after all, be different from the part they were allocated in the audition).

Answering essay questions

FOCUS

- To provide general advice on questions asked at exam level.

Introduction

Examiners set questions to find out how much you know about the subject you have studied. This is true of any of the subjects you study. If you wish to do well, follow the advice on this sheet carefully.

- **Find out as much as you can**
  You are currently studying *An Inspector Calls*. You need to read and reread the play, and you should talk about it as much as you can to other people, especially people who have also read the play, like your teacher and the rest of your class. It will help to have a basic understanding of Britain from just before the First World War to just after the Second World War.

- **Present your information correctly**
  Examiners and teachers will take your answers more seriously if you show that you know how to present your information. Remember the following two points.

  – Write in the present tense: for example, **Eric *is* a heavy drinker**, not **Eric *was* a heavy drinker**.
  – Use quotations, but keep them short, and weave them into your sentences so they do not look or sound awkward.

- **Organise what you want to say**
  Have a clear idea of where you are going with your essay. On the whole, a simple but effective way to make your essays clear is to make general points first and then become more specific later. The specific points should become the evidence that supports your argument.

1. The extract below is part of an answer to a question that asked students to write about Sheila Birling's rather childish personality at the opening of the play. It is a good example of writing that is informed, properly presented and well organised. Read the extract.

   Sheila Birling's character develops and changes dramatically through the course of the play. Before the Inspector's visit she behaves in a rather girlish way. She chatters constantly, barely pausing for breath, and her language is full of contemporary slang such as 'squiffy' and 'chump'. The stage directions indicate that the actress portraying her should be 'playful' and 'excited'. Most of all, she obeys without question the words of her father and Gerald. She does not seriously confront Gerald with his absences the previous summer; nor does she think critically about her father's political views.

2. Note down the ways in which the extract follows the advice given.

3. The extract above is about the way Sheila behaves before the Inspector calls. Using the same style of writing as in the essay extract, write a paragraph about Eric's character.

The first paragraph

FOCUS

- To provide advice on writing the first paragraph of an essay.

Introduction

Many students find that starting an essay is the most difficult part of answering essay questions. If you understand your subject, however, and know what you want to say, you should have no difficulty writing your opening paragraph.

- Read the following essay title.

Essay title

Arthur and Sybil Birling are more concerned with avoiding a scandal than with making sure their family behaves properly. Do you agree with this statement?

What you have to do for this essay is show that Arthur and Sybil Birling consider almost anything forgivable, except the crime of being caught. The passage below shows you one way of writing an introduction to this essay.

> The Birlings are preoccupied with making sure that their public image is perfect. This is because they have so much to lose if any misbehaviour becomes public. In fact, they are so concerned with the appearance of perfection that they seem to care less about what goes on in their family than they do about keeping it private.

Analysis

- This introduction has three sentences.
- The first sentence agrees with the statement in the question, but uses different words to do it.
- The second sentence explains why it is that the Birlings behave in the way the statement suggests.
- The third sentence agrees with the statement again, but uses another way of saying it.
- The statements are very general; there is no need in an introduction to say exactly what you are going to say again later on.
- Key linking words/phrases, such as 'in fact' and 'this is because' help organise the sentences.

- Now, take each of the following three titles and write opening paragraphs to accompany them. Two are in the same style as the example. The third is phrased differently, but can be answered in a similar way.

1. 'The Birlings are as guilty as the Inspector tries to make them feel.' Do you agree?
2. 'Both Sheila and Eric Birling change significantly during the course of the play.' What do you think?
3. Write about the roles that lust and greed play in the main events of *An Inspector Calls*.

Using quotations

FOCUS

- To provide advice on using quotations in an essay.

Introduction

There are three key things to remember when you are using quotations.

- Quotations are important because they help to support your ideas with evidence.
- Quotations should be short and to the point.
- Quotations should be woven into your writing so that they form a natural part of your sentence.

- Imagine you are writing an essay in which you have to show that Sheila is more affected by the Inspector's visit than her parents. You could find quotations, such as those below, to help you do it.

"Oh – how horrible!"
"I think it was a mean thing to do."
"I know I'm to blame – and I'm desperately sorry."

- On their own, these quotations do not mean very much at all. They are only useful once you make something of them. The passage below is an example of one way you can do this. As you are reading, notice how these short quotations support the main ideas in the passage and are introduced into the sentences in a natural way.

Unlike her parents, Sheila has an immediate reaction to the news of Eva's death that shows her shock and concern. When she hears that a young woman has died from drinking disinfectant, she exclaims, **"Oh – how horrible!"**. This mood of shock dominates her feelings and may be partly responsible for the way she turns against her father when she learns of his part in Eva's suicide. She tells him that sacking the girl **"was a mean thing to do"** despite the fact he himself is unwilling to accept any of the blame. For her own part, however, when she discovers the truth about her involvement, she is fully prepared to accept responsibility for having Eva sacked from Milwards. She says guiltily, **"I know I'm to blame – and I'm desperately sorry."**

1. Now, find three quotations to show that Eric too is greatly affected by the Inspector's visit.

2. When you have done this, write a passage, like the one above about Eric.

How men are

FOCUS

- To write an essay on the roles of the men in the play.

Essay title

Write about the ways in which Birling, Eric and Gerald view women.

Planning

- **Stage 1:** Working in small groups of no more than four, first decide whether you will look at Eric or Gerald. Using the points below, make detailed notes about your character.

  - How the character treats Mrs Birling and Sheila Birling.
  - How he treats women (as far as we know) outside the family.
  - How he feels about the way he has treated women after he has spoken to the Inspector.
  - What he says about women during the course of the play.

- **Stage 2:** When your group has finished working, elect a spokesperson and report your findings. Listen to what other groups have to say about the character they have studied. As they are talking, note down what they have discovered.

  You should now have a clearer picture of the way Eric and Gerald see women. They behave well to certain women and they behave badly to others. The way they act in public is generally different to the way they behave in private.

- **Stage 3:** The extract below outlines **some** of Birling's attitudes towards women.

  On the surface, Birling appears to have a positive attitude towards women. He treats his wife and daughter properly and is obviously concerned for their welfare. He hopes that Sheila will be contented with Gerald, but there is a suspicion that Arthur is happy with the marriage mainly because it will mean a better business relationship with Gerald's father. In fact, Mrs Birling has to tell him during his speech of congratulation not to "talk business on an occasion like this". Furthermore, although Arthur Birling appears to want the best for his daughter, he is prepared to forgive Gerald's betrayal of her rather too quickly. He even starts to say that "a lot of young men" in Gerald's situation would behave in the same way.

- Now, write your essay. First, complete the above extract by providing further information, and by writing about the way Birling treats Eva, then write a paragraph for Eric and one for Gerald. Try to write in the same style as above.

Women's roles

FOCUS

- To write an essay on the roles of the women in the play.

Essay title

The women in *An Inspector Calls* are portrayed as having little or no power. Do you agree with this comment?

Planning

- **Stage 1:** Go through the points in the box below. For each of them, write out in note form whether or not the woman being discussed is *exercising* power or *showing a lack of it* at that particular moment. The first point is covered in the example extract.

– Eva is an important person in the strike, but then she is sacked.
– Eva gets a job in a dress shop, but is sacked for upsetting Sheila.
– Eva has no money and no job. Gerald looks after her, then makes her his mistress.
– Eric takes advantage of Eva's miserable situation. He makes her pregnant and she refuses to accept any more of his money when she discovers it is stolen.
– Eva asks Mrs Birling's committee for help but is refused.
– Eva commits suicide.

– Sheila is 'rather excited' and 'playful' before the Inspector arrives.
– Sheila's family tries to protect her from nasty facts about the real world.
– Sheila gets Eva sacked.
– When Sheila discovers the truth about Gerald she breaks off the engagement.
– When Sheila realises what she and her family have done to Eva Smith, she is not afraid to say exactly what she thinks about it.

– Mrs Birling leaves responsibility for important decisions to her husband.
– Mrs Birling has some control over her family.
– Mrs Birling is important in the Brumley Women's Charity Organisation.

- **Stage 2:** Read this example extract that covers the first point above.

Eva Smith appears to have exercised some power, however briefly, during the strike at Birling's factory. She was one of the "four or five ring-leaders" who was trying to get rates of pay increased. Eric says that she must have had a "bit more spirit than the others" and is impressed by what he hears of her. Nevertheless, Eva's spirit is not enough to carry the strike and it soon collapses. She is then quickly shown the cost of speaking out when Arthur Birling sacks her.

- Now, write up your notes as a series of paragraphs in a complete essay, adding an introduction, and a conclusion in which you say whether or not you agree with the statement in the essay title.

Parents and children

FOCUS

- To write an essay about the relationships between the parents and children in the Birling family.

Essay title

Consider the way that the members of the Birling family behave towards each other.

Planning

- **Stage 1:** For this essay you should look at whether Arthur and Sybil Birling can be considered good parents and whether Eric and Sheila behave as good children. Either individually or in pairs, write down five good characteristics you think it is important for parents to have. Then write down five characteristics you think parents should try to avoid. When you have written these down, try to think of instances in which parents display the types of behaviour you have described. Finally, discuss your ideas with the rest of the class. Are there any characteristics that have been mentioned a lot?

Good characteristics	Bad characteristics
1.	1.
2.	2.
3.	3.
4.	4.
5.	5.

- **Stage 2:** Now, think about Arthur and Sybil Birling. Write down instances of their attitude towards Eric and Sheila. Say whether each example shows a negative or a positive aspect of their characters.
- **Stage 3:** Finally, consider the behaviour of Eric and Sheila. Do they treat their parents as they should? Write down as many examples as you can and then report your findings back to the class.

- Now write your essay. In your essay, you should write about:
  - Arthur's attitude towards Eric's general behaviour
  - Eric's actions when he gets into trouble with Eva
  - Sybil's treatment of Sheila and her relationship with Eric
  - the way that Sheila responds to both her parents.

Scandal!

FOCUS

- To write an essay on scandal and hypocrisy in the play.

Essay title

Arthur and Sybil Birling are more concerned with avoiding a scandal than with making sure their family behaves properly. Do you agree with this comment?

Planning

- **Stage 1:** You need to show the way the Birlings react to the Inspector's revelations about their family. To help you do this, read the points below.

  – Eric has stolen money from the Birling family business. He has also made a young woman pregnant and left her to deal with the consequences. Mr and Mrs Birling are shocked to hear what he has done and are afraid his actions will become public knowledge.

  – Gerald has cheated on their daughter. They forgive him almost immediately and encourage Sheila to do the same.

  – Mr and Mrs Birling are completely unwilling to accept that their actions have anything to do with Eva Smith's death.

  – When the Birlings discover the Inspector is not on the local police force they are delighted. They cannot accept that what he had to say was important, whoever he was.

  As a class, discuss these points one by one. Say how you think each of them demonstrates the way the Birlings are more concerned about scandal than the manner in which their family has behaved.

- **Stage 2:** Now, write at least one paragraph for each of the four points above, adding any points made during the discussion. This will form the main part of your answer to the essay question, but feel free to add any more ideas if you wish.

- Now, write your essay. Starting with Eric, write a paragraph or two in which you refer to the Birlings' reactions to the pregnancy. In addition, look for information on Birling's feelings about the theft of money. What is it that really upsets him?

Exam passage

- Read this passage carefully and then answer all the questions that follow.

GERALD **The girl saw me looking at her and then gave me a glance that was nothing less than a cry for help. So I went across and told Joe Meggarty some nonsense – that the manager had a message for him or something like that – got him out of the way – and then told the girl that if she didn't want any more of that sort of thing, she'd better let me take her out of there. She agreed at once.**

INSPECTOR **Where did you go?**

GERALD **We went along to the County Hotel, which I knew would be quiet at that time of night, and we had a drink or two and talked.**

INSPECTOR **Did she drink much at that time?**

GERALD **No. She only had a port and lemonade – or some such concoction. All she wanted was to talk – a little friendliness – and I gathered that Joe Meggarty's advances had left her rather shaken – as well they might –**

INSPECTOR **She talked about herself?**

GERALD **Yes. I asked her questions about herself. She told me her name was Daisy Renton, that she'd lost both parents, that she came originally from somewhere outside Brumley. She also told me she'd had a job in one of the works here and had had to leave after a strike. She said something about the shop too, but wouldn't say which it was, and she was deliberately vague about what happened. I couldn't get any exact details from her about her past life. She wanted to talk about herself – just because she felt I was interested and friendly – but at the same time she wanted to be Daisy Renton – and not Eva Smith. In fact, I heard that name for the first time tonight. What she did let slip – though she didn't mean to – was that she was desperately hard up and at that moment was actually hungry. I made the people at the County find some food for her.**

These questions are all based on the passage.

1. Why does Gerald first become interested in Eva Smith?
2. Gerald is describing the first time he meets Eva. Why was she so desperate at this point? Write out **three phrases** that show her sense of desperation.
3. Write about how the conduct of Gerald and Eva in this scene is rather better than that of most of the other characters in the rest of the play. Write out **three phrases** that show this.

This question is based on the novel as a whole.

4. Imagine you are Sheila listening to Gerald's account of the beginning of his affair. Write down your thoughts and feelings about the way he has behaved. You should not take a completely negative view of his behaviour.

Selected answers

Guess who? (Page 7)

1. a. Birling
   b. Mrs Birling
   c. Gerald
   d. Sheila
   e. Eric
   f. Inspector

2. a. Mrs Birling
   b. Inspector
   c. Birling
   d. Eric
   e. Sheila
   f. Gerald

Who says? (Page 14)

1. a. Inspector
   b. Eric
   c. Inspector
   d. Gerald
   e. Birling
   f. Sheila
   g. Mrs Birling
   h. Sheila

Crossword (Page 15)

1 E	N	2 G	A	G	E	3 M	E	4 N	T	5 R	I	N	6 G	
		O				A		A		E			E	
7 C	O	L	D			Y		8 M	Y	S	T	E	R	Y
R		F			9 G	O	O	L	E	P			A	
O						R				O			L	
10 F	A	M	I	11 L	Y		12 D	R	I	N	K		D	
T				E			U			S		13 M		
S		14 D	R	A	M	A	T	I	C	I	R	O	N	Y
				D			Y			B		N		
15 P			16 F	E	A	R		17 K	A	I	S	E	R	
R		18 D		R			19 S			L		Y		20 G
I		R			21 T	I	T	A	N	I	C			R
22 D	I	A	R	23 Y			E			T		24 E		E
E		M		E		25 P	A	R	T	Y		V		E
	26 D	A	I	S	Y		L				27 M	A	I	D

The road to suicide (Page 21)

3	6	2
9	1	4
5	7	8